This book belongs to:

_____

ANIMAL:

ANIMAL CLASS:

☐ MAMMAL ☐ AMPHIBIAN ☐ FISH ☐ BIRD ☐ REPTILE ☐ INVERTEBRATE

FOOD

HABITAT

SIZE

MY FAVORITE THING ABOUT THIS ANIMAL IS:

FIELD NOTES:

ANIMAL:

ANIMAL CLASS:

☐ MAMMAL ☐ AMPHIBIAN ☐ FISH ☐ BIRD ☐ REPTILE ☐ INVERTEBRATE

FOOD

HABITAT

SIZE

MY FAVORITE THING ABOUT THIS ANIMAL IS:

FIELD NOTES:

ANIMAL:

ANIMAL CLASS:

☐ MAMMAL ☐ AMPHIBIAN ☐ FISH ☐ BIRD ☐ REPTILE ☐ INVERTEBRATE

FOOD

HABITAT

SIZE

MY FAVORITE THING ABOUT THIS ANIMAL IS:

FIELD NOTES:

ANIMAL:

ANIMAL CLASS:

☐ MAMMAL   ☐ AMPHIBIAN   ☐ FISH   ☐ BIRD   ☐ REPTILE   ☐ INVERTEBRATE

FOOD

HABITAT

SIZE

MY FAVORITE THING ABOUT THIS ANIMAL IS:

FIELD NOTES:

ANIMAL:

ANIMAL CLASS:

☐ MAMMAL   ☐ AMPHIBIAN   ☐ FISH   ☐ BIRD   ☐ REPTILE   ☐ INVERTEBRATE

FOOD

HABITAT

SIZE

MY FAVORITE THING ABOUT THIS ANIMAL IS:

FIELD NOTES:

ANIMAL:

ANIMAL CLASS:

☐ MAMMAL   ☐ AMPHIBIAN   ☐ FISH   ☐ BIRD   ☐ REPTILE   ☐ INVERTEBRATE

FOOD

HABITAT

SIZE

MY FAVORITE THING ABOUT THIS ANIMAL IS:

FIELD NOTES:

ANIMAL:

ANIMAL CLASS:

☐ MAMMAL   ☐ AMPHIBIAN   ☐ FISH   ☐ BIRD   ☐ REPTILE   ☐ INVERTEBRATE

FOOD

HABITAT

SIZE

MY FAVORITE THING ABOUT THIS ANIMAL IS:

FIELD NOTES:

ANIMAL:

ANIMAL CLASS:

☐ MAMMAL   ☐ AMPHIBIAN   ☐ FISH   ☐ BIRD   ☐ REPTILE   ☐ INVERTEBRATE

FOOD

HABITAT

SIZE

MY FAVORITE THING ABOUT THIS ANIMAL IS:

FIELD NOTES:

ANIMAL:

ANIMAL CLASS:

☐ MAMMAL ☐ AMPHIBIAN ☐ FISH ☐ BIRD ☐ REPTILE ☐ INVERTEBRATE

FOOD

HABITAT

SIZE

MY FAVORITE THING ABOUT THIS ANIMAL IS:

FIELD NOTES:

ANIMAL:

ANIMAL CLASS:

☐ MAMMAL ☐ AMPHIBIAN ☐ FISH ☐ BIRD ☐ REPTILE ☐ INVERTEBRATE

FOOD

HABITAT

SIZE

MY FAVORITE THING ABOUT THIS ANIMAL IS:

FIELD NOTES:

ANIMAL:

ANIMAL CLASS:

☐ MAMMAL ☐ AMPHIBIAN ☐ FISH ☐ BIRD ☐ REPTILE ☐ INVERTEBRATE

FOOD

HABITAT

SIZE

MY FAVORITE THING ABOUT THIS ANIMAL IS:

FIELD NOTES:

ANIMAL:

ANIMAL CLASS:

☐ MAMMAL ☐ AMPHIBIAN ☐ FISH ☐ BIRD ☐ REPTILE ☐ INVERTEBRATE

FOOD

HABITAT

SIZE

MY FAVORITE THING ABOUT THIS ANIMAL IS:

FIELD NOTES:

ANIMAL:

ANIMAL CLASS:

☐ MAMMAL　☐ AMPHIBIAN　☐ FISH　☐ BIRD　☐ REPTILE　☐ INVERTEBRATE

FOOD

HABITAT

SIZE

MY FAVORITE THING ABOUT THIS ANIMAL IS:

FIELD NOTES:

ANIMAL:

ANIMAL CLASS:

☐ MAMMAL ☐ AMPHIBIAN ☐ FISH ☐ BIRD ☐ REPTILE ☐ INVERTEBRATE

FOOD

HABITAT

SIZE

MY FAVORITE THING ABOUT THIS ANIMAL IS:

FIELD NOTES:

ANIMAL:

ANIMAL CLASS:

☐ MAMMAL   ☐ AMPHIBIAN   ☐ FISH   ☐ BIRD   ☐ REPTILE   ☐ INVERTEBRATE

FOOD

HABITAT

SIZE

MY FAVORITE THING ABOUT THIS ANIMAL IS:

FIELD NOTES:

ANIMAL:

ANIMAL CLASS:

☐ MAMMAL   ☐ AMPHIBIAN   ☐ FISH   ☐ BIRD   ☐ REPTILE   ☐ INVERTEBRATE

FOOD

HABITAT

SIZE

MY FAVORITE THING ABOUT THIS ANIMAL IS:

FIELD NOTES:

ANIMAL:

ANIMAL CLASS:

☐ MAMMAL ☐ AMPHIBIAN ☐ FISH ☐ BIRD ☐ REPTILE ☐ INVERTEBRATE

FOOD

HABITAT

SIZE

MY FAVORITE THING ABOUT THIS ANIMAL IS:

FIELD NOTES:

ANIMAL:

ANIMAL CLASS:

☐ MAMMAL   ☐ AMPHIBIAN   ☐ FISH   ☐ BIRD   ☐ REPTILE   ☐ INVERTEBRATE

FOOD

HABITAT

SIZE

MY FAVORITE THING ABOUT THIS ANIMAL IS:

FIELD NOTES:

ANIMAL:

ANIMAL CLASS:

☐ MAMMAL ☐ AMPHIBIAN ☐ FISH ☐ BIRD ☐ REPTILE ☐ INVERTEBRATE

FOOD

HABITAT

SIZE

MY FAVORITE THING ABOUT THIS ANIMAL IS:

FIELD NOTES:

ANIMAL:

ANIMAL CLASS:
☐ MAMMAL   ☐ AMPHIBIAN   ☐ FISH   ☐ BIRD   ☐ REPTILE   ☐ INVERTEBRATE

FOOD

HABITAT

SIZE

MY FAVORITE THING ABOUT THIS ANIMAL IS:

FIELD NOTES:

ANIMAL:

ANIMAL CLASS:
☐ MAMMAL ☐ AMPHIBIAN ☐ FISH ☐ BIRD ☐ REPTILE ☐ INVERTEBRATE

FOOD

HABITAT

SIZE

MY FAVORITE THING ABOUT THIS ANIMAL IS:

FIELD NOTES:

ANIMAL:

ANIMAL CLASS:

☐ MAMMAL   ☐ AMPHIBIAN   ☐ FISH   ☐ BIRD   ☐ REPTILE   ☐ INVERTEBRATE

FOOD

HABITAT

SIZE

MY FAVORITE THING ABOUT THIS ANIMAL IS:

FIELD NOTES:

ANIMAL:

ANIMAL CLASS:

☐ MAMMAL ☐ AMPHIBIAN ☐ FISH ☐ BIRD ☐ REPTILE ☐ INVERTEBRATE

FOOD

HABITAT

SIZE

MY FAVORITE THING ABOUT THIS ANIMAL IS:

FIELD NOTES:

ANIMAL:

ANIMAL CLASS:

☐ MAMMAL ☐ AMPHIBIAN ☐ FISH ☐ BIRD ☐ REPTILE ☐ INVERTEBRATE

FOOD

HABITAT

SIZE

MY FAVORITE THING ABOUT THIS ANIMAL IS:

FIELD NOTES:

ANIMAL:

ANIMAL CLASS:

☐ MAMMAL ☐ AMPHIBIAN ☐ FISH ☐ BIRD ☐ REPTILE ☐ INVERTEBRATE

FOOD

HABITAT

SIZE

MY FAVORITE THING ABOUT THIS ANIMAL IS:

FIELD NOTES:

ANIMAL:

ANIMAL CLASS:

☐ MAMMAL ☐ AMPHIBIAN ☐ FISH ☐ BIRD ☐ REPTILE ☐ INVERTEBRATE

FOOD

HABITAT

SIZE

MY FAVORITE THING ABOUT THIS ANIMAL IS:

FIELD NOTES:

ANIMAL:

ANIMAL CLASS:

☐ MAMMAL   ☐ AMPHIBIAN   ☐ FISH   ☐ BIRD   ☐ REPTILE   ☐ INVERTEBRATE

FOOD

HABITAT

SIZE

MY FAVORITE THING ABOUT THIS ANIMAL IS:

FIELD NOTES:

ANIMAL:

ANIMAL CLASS:

☐ MAMMAL   ☐ AMPHIBIAN   ☐ FISH   ☐ BIRD   ☐ REPTILE   ☐ INVERTEBRATE

FOOD

HABITAT

SIZE

MY FAVORITE THING ABOUT THIS ANIMAL IS:

FIELD NOTES:

ANIMAL:

ANIMAL CLASS:
☐ MAMMAL ☐ AMPHIBIAN ☐ FISH ☐ BIRD ☐ REPTILE ☐ INVERTEBRATE

FOOD

HABITAT

SIZE

MY FAVORITE THING ABOUT THIS ANIMAL IS:

FIELD NOTES:

ANIMAL:

ANIMAL CLASS:

☐ MAMMAL ☐ AMPHIBIAN ☐ FISH ☐ BIRD ☐ REPTILE ☐ INVERTEBRATE

FOOD

HABITAT

SIZE

MY FAVORITE THING ABOUT THIS ANIMAL IS:

FIELD NOTES:

ANIMAL:

ANIMAL CLASS:

☐ MAMMAL ☐ AMPHIBIAN ☐ FISH ☐ BIRD ☐ REPTILE ☐ INVERTEBRATE

FOOD

HABITAT

SIZE

MY FAVORITE THING ABOUT THIS ANIMAL IS:

FIELD NOTES:

ANIMAL:

ANIMAL CLASS:

☐ MAMMAL ☐ AMPHIBIAN ☐ FISH ☐ BIRD ☐ REPTILE ☐ INVERTEBRATE

FOOD

HABITAT

SIZE

MY FAVORITE THING ABOUT THIS ANIMAL IS:

FIELD NOTES:

ANIMAL:

ANIMAL CLASS:

☐ MAMMAL ☐ AMPHIBIAN ☐ FISH ☐ BIRD ☐ REPTILE ☐ INVERTEBRATE

FOOD

HABITAT

SIZE

MY FAVORITE THING ABOUT THIS ANIMAL IS:

FIELD NOTES:

ANIMAL:

ANIMAL CLASS:

☐ MAMMAL ☐ AMPHIBIAN ☐ FISH ☐ BIRD ☐ REPTILE ☐ INVERTEBRATE

FOOD

HABITAT

SIZE

MY FAVORITE THING ABOUT THIS ANIMAL IS:

FIELD NOTES:

ANIMAL:

ANIMAL CLASS:

☐ MAMMAL   ☐ AMPHIBIAN   ☐ FISH   ☐ BIRD   ☐ REPTILE   ☐ INVERTEBRATE

FOOD

HABITAT

SIZE

MY FAVORITE THING ABOUT THIS ANIMAL IS:

FIELD NOTES:

ANIMAL:

ANIMAL CLASS:

☐ MAMMAL ☐ AMPHIBIAN ☐ FISH ☐ BIRD ☐ REPTILE ☐ INVERTEBRATE

FOOD

HABITAT

SIZE

MY FAVORITE THING ABOUT THIS ANIMAL IS:

FIELD NOTES:

ANIMAL:

ANIMAL CLASS:

☐ MAMMAL ☐ AMPHIBIAN ☐ FISH ☐ BIRD ☐ REPTILE ☐ INVERTEBRATE

FOOD

HABITAT

SIZE

MY FAVORITE THING ABOUT THIS ANIMAL IS:

FIELD NOTES:

ANIMAL:

ANIMAL CLASS:

☐ MAMMAL   ☐ AMPHIBIAN   ☐ FISH   ☐ BIRD   ☐ REPTILE   ☐ INVERTEBRATE

FOOD

HABITAT

SIZE

MY FAVORITE THING ABOUT THIS ANIMAL IS:

FIELD NOTES:

ANIMAL:

ANIMAL CLASS:

☐ MAMMAL   ☐ AMPHIBIAN   ☐ FISH   ☐ BIRD   ☐ REPTILE   ☐ INVERTEBRATE

FOOD

HABITAT

SIZE

MY FAVORITE THING ABOUT THIS ANIMAL IS:

FIELD NOTES:

ANIMAL:

ANIMAL CLASS:

☐ MAMMAL ☐ AMPHIBIAN ☐ FISH ☐ BIRD ☐ REPTILE ☐ INVERTEBRATE

FOOD

HABITAT

SIZE

MY FAVORITE THING ABOUT THIS ANIMAL IS:

FIELD NOTES:

ANIMAL:

ANIMAL CLASS:

☐ MAMMAL ☐ AMPHIBIAN ☐ FISH ☐ BIRD ☐ REPTILE ☐ INVERTEBRATE

FOOD

HABITAT

SIZE

MY FAVORITE THING ABOUT THIS ANIMAL IS:

FIELD NOTES:

ANIMAL:

ANIMAL CLASS:

☐ MAMMAL ☐ AMPHIBIAN ☐ FISH ☐ BIRD ☐ REPTILE ☐ INVERTEBRATE

FOOD

HABITAT

SIZE

MY FAVORITE THING ABOUT THIS ANIMAL IS:

FIELD NOTES:

ANIMAL:

ANIMAL CLASS:

☐ MAMMAL ☐ AMPHIBIAN ☐ FISH ☐ BIRD ☐ REPTILE ☐ INVERTEBRATE

FOOD

HABITAT

SIZE

MY FAVORITE THING ABOUT THIS ANIMAL IS:

FIELD NOTES:

ANIMAL:

ANIMAL CLASS:

☐ MAMMAL ☐ AMPHIBIAN ☐ FISH ☐ BIRD ☐ REPTILE ☐ INVERTEBRATE

FOOD

HABITAT

SIZE

MY FAVORITE THING ABOUT THIS ANIMAL IS:

FIELD NOTES:

ANIMAL:

ANIMAL CLASS:

☐ MAMMAL ☐ AMPHIBIAN ☐ FISH ☐ BIRD ☐ REPTILE ☐ INVERTEBRATE

FOOD

HABITAT

SIZE

MY FAVORITE THING ABOUT THIS ANIMAL IS:

FIELD NOTES:

ANIMAL:

ANIMAL CLASS:

☐ MAMMAL ☐ AMPHIBIAN ☐ FISH ☐ BIRD ☐ REPTILE ☐ INVERTEBRATE

FOOD

HABITAT

SIZE

MY FAVORITE THING ABOUT THIS ANIMAL IS:

FIELD NOTES:

ANIMAL:

ANIMAL CLASS:

☐ MAMMAL ☐ AMPHIBIAN ☐ FISH ☐ BIRD ☐ REPTILE ☐ INVERTEBRATE

FOOD

HABITAT

SIZE

MY FAVORITE THING ABOUT THIS ANIMAL IS:

FIELD NOTES:

ANIMAL:

ANIMAL CLASS:

☐ MAMMAL   ☐ AMPHIBIAN   ☐ FISH   ☐ BIRD   ☐ REPTILE   ☐ INVERTEBRATE

FOOD

HABITAT

SIZE

MY FAVORITE THING ABOUT THIS ANIMAL IS:

FIELD NOTES:

ANIMAL:

ANIMAL CLASS:

☐ MAMMAL ☐ AMPHIBIAN ☐ FISH ☐ BIRD ☐ REPTILE ☐ INVERTEBRATE

FOOD

HABITAT

SIZE

MY FAVORITE THING ABOUT THIS ANIMAL IS:

FIELD NOTES:

ANIMAL:

ANIMAL CLASS:

☐ MAMMAL   ☐ AMPHIBIAN   ☐ FISH   ☐ BIRD   ☐ REPTILE   ☐ INVERTEBRATE

FOOD

HABITAT

SIZE

MY FAVORITE THING ABOUT THIS ANIMAL IS:

FIELD NOTES:

Made in United States
Orlando, FL
20 December 2024

56140242R10057